50 Japanese BBQ and Beyond Recipes

By: Kelly Johnson

Table of Contents

- Yakiniku (Japanese Grilled Meat)
- Miso-Marinated Grilled Chicken
- Wagyu Steak with Ponzu Sauce
- Teriyaki Glazed Short Ribs
- Shioyaki Salmon (Salt-Grilled Salmon)
- Yakitori (Grilled Chicken Skewers)
- Negima Yakitori (Chicken and Green Onion Skewers)
- Tsukune (Chicken Meatball Skewers)
- Buta Bara (Pork Belly Skewers)
- Yaki Onigiri (Grilled Rice Balls)
- Miso Butter Corn on the Grill
- Japanese-Style Grilled Eggplant (Nasu Dengaku)
- Gindara Saikyo Yaki (Miso-Marinated Black Cod)
- Unagi Kabayaki (Grilled Eel)
- Grilled Squid with Soy Sauce
- Saba Shioyaki (Grilled Mackerel with Salt)
- Gyu Kushi (Beef Skewers)
- Teba Shio (Salted Grilled Chicken Wings)
- Hotate Yaki (Grilled Scallops)
- Ebi Yaki (Grilled Prawns with Soy Sauce)
- Japanese-Style BBQ Pork Ribs
- Gyu Tan (Grilled Beef Tongue)
- Horumon Yaki (Grilled Offal)
- Shishamo Yaki (Grilled Smelt Fish)
- Miso-Grilled Mushrooms
- Grilled Tofu with Yuzu Miso Glaze
- Okonomiyaki on the Grill
- Yaki Tomorokoshi (Grilled Corn with Miso Butter)
- Teppanyaki Garlic Shrimp
- Yakisoba (Grilled Stir-Fried Noodles)
- Japanese-Style BBQ Lamb Chops
- Sesame Soy Grilled Asparagus
- Grilled Daikon with Soy Sauce and Bonito Flakes
- Shabu Shabu Grilled Pork Belly Wraps
- Japanese-Style BBQ Duck Breast

- Gyudon-Style Grilled Beef Bowl
- Yakionigiri with Spicy Tuna Topping
- Sansho Pepper Grilled Chicken Thighs
- Gochujang-Miso BBQ Glaze for Meats
- Spicy Mentaiko Mayo Grilled Seafood
- Teppanyaki-Style Garlic Butter Vegetables
- Japanese BBQ Glazed Eggplant Skewers
- Grilled Mochi with Sweet Soy Sauce
- Wasabi-Soy Grilled Ahi Tuna
- Teriyaki Lamb Skewers
- Grilled Chicken Gizzard Skewers
- Miso-Marinated Grilled Tofu Steaks
- Charred Green Peppers with Bonito Flakes
- Japanese BBQ Ramen with Smoked Pork
- Smoked Bonito with Citrus Soy Glaze

Yakiniku (Japanese Grilled Meat)

Ingredients:

- 1 lb thinly sliced beef (ribeye, short ribs, or sirloin)
- 1/4 cup soy sauce
- 2 tbsp mirin
- 2 tbsp sake
- 1 tbsp sesame oil
- 1 tbsp sugar
- 2 cloves garlic, minced
- 1 tsp grated ginger
- 1 tbsp toasted sesame seeds
- 2 green onions, chopped

Instructions:

1. Mix soy sauce, mirin, sake, sesame oil, sugar, garlic, and ginger in a bowl.
2. Marinate beef for at least 30 minutes.
3. Grill over high heat for 1–2 minutes per side.
4. Sprinkle with sesame seeds and green onions before serving.

Miso-Marinated Grilled Chicken

Ingredients:

- 2 boneless chicken thighs
- 3 tbsp white miso paste
- 2 tbsp mirin
- 1 tbsp sake
- 1 tbsp sugar
- 1 tsp soy sauce
- 1 tsp grated ginger

Instructions:

1. Mix miso, mirin, sake, sugar, soy sauce, and ginger into a marinade.
2. Coat chicken and marinate for 3 hours or overnight.
3. Grill over medium heat for 6–7 minutes per side until golden.
4. Serve with steamed rice and pickled vegetables.

Wagyu Steak with Ponzu Sauce

Ingredients:

- 1 lb Wagyu steak (ribeye or striploin)
- 1/4 cup ponzu sauce
- 1 tbsp grated daikon radish
- 1 tsp yuzu juice (optional)
- 1 green onion, sliced

Instructions:

1. Let steak rest at room temperature for 30 minutes.
2. Sear over high heat for 2–3 minutes per side. Let rest for 5 minutes.
3. Slice and serve with ponzu sauce, grated daikon, yuzu juice, and green onions.

Teriyaki Glazed Short Ribs

Ingredients:

- 1 lb beef short ribs
- 1/4 cup soy sauce
- 2 tbsp mirin
- 2 tbsp sake
- 2 tbsp honey
- 1 tbsp grated garlic
- 1 tbsp grated ginger
- 1 tsp cornstarch (mixed with 1 tbsp water)

Instructions:

1. Mix soy sauce, mirin, sake, honey, garlic, and ginger. Marinate ribs for at least 2 hours.
2. Grill over medium-high heat for 3–4 minutes per side.
3. Simmer remaining marinade with cornstarch until thickened.
4. Brush ribs with glaze before serving.

Shioyaki Salmon (Salt-Grilled Salmon)

Ingredients:

- 2 salmon fillets
- 1 tsp sea salt
- Lemon wedges
- Grated daikon radish (optional)

Instructions:

1. Sprinkle salt evenly over salmon and let rest for 15 minutes.
2. Grill over medium heat for 4–5 minutes per side.
3. Serve with lemon wedges and grated daikon.

Yakitori (Grilled Chicken Skewers)

Ingredients:

- 1 lb boneless chicken thighs, cut into cubes
- 1/4 cup soy sauce
- 2 tbsp mirin
- 1 tbsp sake
- 1 tbsp sugar
- 1 tsp grated garlic
- 1 tsp grated ginger
- 1 tbsp vegetable oil

Instructions:

1. Mix soy sauce, mirin, sake, sugar, garlic, and ginger. Marinate chicken for 30 minutes.
2. Thread onto skewers and brush with oil.
3. Grill over medium-high heat for 3–4 minutes per side, brushing with leftover marinade.

Negima Yakitori (Chicken and Green Onion Skewers)

Ingredients:

- 1 lb boneless chicken thighs, cut into cubes
- 4 green onions, cut into 1-inch pieces
- 1/4 cup soy sauce
- 2 tbsp mirin
- 1 tbsp sake
- 1 tbsp honey

Instructions:

1. Mix soy sauce, mirin, sake, and honey for marinade.
2. Thread chicken and green onion alternately onto skewers.
3. Grill over medium heat for 3–4 minutes per side, brushing with marinade.

Tsukune (Chicken Meatball Skewers)

Ingredients:

- 1 lb ground chicken
- 1 egg
- 2 tbsp panko breadcrumbs
- 1 tbsp soy sauce
- 1 tbsp mirin
- 1 tsp grated ginger
- 1 tbsp vegetable oil

For Glaze:

- 1/4 cup soy sauce
- 2 tbsp mirin
- 1 tbsp sugar

Instructions:

1. Mix chicken, egg, panko, soy sauce, mirin, and ginger. Shape into small meatballs.
2. Grill over medium heat for 3 minutes per side.
3. Simmer glaze ingredients until thickened. Brush over meatballs before serving.

Buta Bara (Pork Belly Skewers)

Ingredients:

- 1 lb pork belly, sliced into 1-inch cubes
- 1/4 cup soy sauce
- 2 tbsp mirin
- 1 tbsp sake
- 1 tbsp sugar
- 1 tsp grated garlic
- 1 tsp grated ginger

Instructions:

1. Mix soy sauce, mirin, sake, sugar, garlic, and ginger. Marinate pork belly for 30 minutes.
2. Thread onto skewers.
3. Grill over medium-high heat for 3–4 minutes per side, brushing with leftover marinade.

Yaki Onigiri (Grilled Rice Balls)

Ingredients:

- 2 cups cooked Japanese short-grain rice
- 2 tbsp soy sauce
- 1 tbsp miso paste (optional)
- 1 tbsp mirin
- 1 tbsp butter (optional)
- 1 tbsp sesame oil

Instructions:

1. Wet hands and shape rice into firm triangular or round balls.
2. Mix soy sauce, miso, and mirin.
3. Grill on medium heat, brushing with sauce, for 3–4 minutes per side until crispy.

Miso Butter Corn on the Grill

Ingredients:

- 2 ears of corn
- 2 tbsp butter, melted
- 1 tbsp white miso paste
- 1 tbsp soy sauce
- 1 tsp honey

Instructions:

1. Mix butter, miso, soy sauce, and honey.
2. Grill corn over medium heat, turning occasionally.
3. Brush with miso butter in the last 2 minutes of grilling.

Japanese-Style Grilled Eggplant (Nasu Dengaku)

Ingredients:

- 2 Japanese eggplants, halved lengthwise
- 2 tbsp miso paste
- 1 tbsp mirin
- 1 tbsp sake
- 1 tsp sugar
- 1 tbsp sesame seeds (for garnish)

Instructions:

1. Score the eggplant flesh and grill cut-side down for 3–4 minutes.
2. Mix miso, mirin, sake, and sugar.
3. Flip eggplants, brush with miso glaze, and grill for another 2 minutes.
4. Garnish with sesame seeds before serving.

Gindara Saikyo Yaki (Miso-Marinated Black Cod)

Ingredients:

- 2 black cod fillets
- 1/4 cup white miso paste
- 2 tbsp sake
- 2 tbsp mirin
- 1 tbsp sugar

Instructions:

1. Mix miso, sake, mirin, and sugar. Marinate fish for 24–48 hours.
2. Wipe off excess marinade and grill over medium heat for 4–5 minutes per side.

Unagi Kabayaki (Grilled Eel with Sweet Soy Glaze)

Ingredients:

- 2 eel fillets
- 1/4 cup soy sauce
- 2 tbsp mirin
- 2 tbsp sake
- 1 tbsp sugar

Instructions:

1. Heat soy sauce, mirin, sake, and sugar until slightly thickened.
2. Grill eel over medium heat for 3–4 minutes per side.
3. Brush with sauce and grill for 1 more minute.

Grilled Squid with Soy Sauce

Ingredients:

- 1 whole squid, cleaned
- 1/4 cup soy sauce
- 2 tbsp mirin
- 1 tbsp sake
- 1 tsp grated ginger

Instructions:

1. Mix soy sauce, mirin, sake, and ginger. Marinate squid for 30 minutes.
2. Grill over medium-high heat for 2–3 minutes per side.
3. Brush with more marinade before serving.

Saba Shioyaki (Grilled Mackerel with Salt)

Ingredients:

- 2 mackerel fillets
- 1 tsp sea salt
- Lemon wedges

Instructions:

1. Sprinkle salt on mackerel and let rest for 15 minutes.
2. Grill over medium-high heat for 4–5 minutes per side.
3. Serve with lemon wedges.

Gyu Kushi (Beef Skewers)

Ingredients:

- 1 lb beef (sirloin or ribeye), cut into cubes
- 1/4 cup soy sauce
- 2 tbsp sake
- 1 tbsp mirin
- 1 tbsp sugar
- 1 tsp grated garlic

Instructions:

1. Mix soy sauce, sake, mirin, sugar, and garlic. Marinate beef for 30 minutes.
2. Thread onto skewers.
3. Grill over medium-high heat for 2–3 minutes per side.

Teba Shio (Salted Grilled Chicken Wings)

Ingredients:

- 8 chicken wings
- 1 tsp sea salt
- 1/2 tsp black pepper
- 1/2 tsp sake
- Lemon wedges

Instructions:

1. Pat chicken wings dry and season with salt, pepper, and sake. Let rest for 15 minutes.
2. Grill over medium-high heat for 6–8 minutes per side until crispy.
3. Serve with lemon wedges.

Hotate Yaki (Grilled Scallops)

Ingredients:

- 6 fresh scallops
- 2 tbsp soy sauce
- 1 tbsp mirin
- 1 tbsp butter
- 1 tsp grated garlic

Instructions:

1. Mix soy sauce, mirin, and garlic.
2. Grill scallops over medium-high heat for 2 minutes per side.
3. Brush with sauce and top with butter before serving.

Ebi Yaki (Grilled Prawns with Soy Sauce)

Ingredients:

- 6 large prawns
- 2 tbsp soy sauce
- 1 tbsp sake
- 1 tbsp butter
- 1 clove garlic, minced

Instructions:

1. Mix soy sauce, sake, and garlic. Marinate prawns for 15 minutes.
2. Grill over medium-high heat for 2–3 minutes per side.
3. Brush with butter before serving.

Japanese-Style BBQ Pork Ribs

Ingredients:

- 2 lbs pork ribs
- 1/4 cup soy sauce
- 2 tbsp sake
- 2 tbsp mirin
- 1 tbsp honey
- 1 tbsp grated garlic
- 1 tbsp grated ginger

Instructions:

1. Mix marinade ingredients and coat ribs. Marinate for at least 3 hours.
2. Grill over low heat for 20 minutes, turning occasionally.
3. Brush with leftover marinade while grilling.

Gyu Tan (Grilled Beef Tongue)

Ingredients:

- 1/2 lb beef tongue, thinly sliced
- 1/2 tsp sea salt
- 1/2 tsp black pepper
- 1 tsp lemon juice
- 1 green onion, chopped

Instructions:

1. Sprinkle beef tongue with salt and pepper.
2. Grill over high heat for 1–2 minutes per side.
3. Serve with lemon juice and green onions.

Horumon Yaki (Grilled Offal)

Ingredients:

- 1 lb beef or pork offal (tripe, intestine, etc.)
- 1/4 cup soy sauce
- 2 tbsp miso paste
- 1 tbsp mirin
- 1 tbsp sesame oil
- 1 tbsp grated garlic
- 1 tbsp grated ginger

Instructions:

1. Clean and blanch offal in boiling water for 5 minutes. Drain.
2. Mix marinade and coat offal. Let rest for 30 minutes.
3. Grill over medium heat for 3–4 minutes per side until charred.

Shishamo Yaki (Grilled Smelt Fish)

Ingredients:

- 6 shishamo (Japanese smelt)
- 1/2 tsp sea salt
- Lemon wedges

Instructions:

1. Sprinkle salt evenly over fish.
2. Grill over medium heat for 3 minutes per side.
3. Serve with lemon wedges.

Miso-Grilled Mushrooms

Ingredients:

- 6 shiitake mushrooms
- 2 tbsp miso paste
- 1 tbsp mirin
- 1 tbsp sake
- 1 tsp sesame oil

Instructions:

1. Mix miso, mirin, sake, and sesame oil.
2. Brush mushrooms with sauce and grill over medium heat for 2–3 minutes per side.

Grilled Tofu with Yuzu Miso Glaze

Ingredients:

- 1 block firm tofu, cut into thick slices
- 2 tbsp white miso
- 1 tbsp yuzu juice
- 1 tbsp mirin
- 1 tsp soy sauce
- 1/2 tsp sesame oil

Instructions:

1. Pat tofu dry and grill over medium heat for 3 minutes per side.
2. Mix miso, yuzu, mirin, soy sauce, and sesame oil.
3. Brush tofu with glaze and grill for 1 more minute.

Okonomiyaki on the Grill (Japanese Savory Pancake)

Ingredients:

- 1 cup all-purpose flour
- 1/2 cup dashi (or water)
- 1 egg
- 1 cup shredded cabbage
- 2 tbsp green onions, chopped
- 1/4 cup cooked bacon or pork belly, sliced
- 2 tbsp okonomiyaki sauce
- 2 tbsp Japanese mayo
- 1 tbsp bonito flakes
- 1 tsp aonori (seaweed flakes)

Instructions:

1. Mix flour, dashi, and egg into a smooth batter.
2. Fold in cabbage, green onions, and bacon.
3. Heat a flat-top grill or griddle, grease with oil, and pour the batter into a round shape.
4. Cook for 4–5 minutes per side until golden brown.
5. Drizzle with okonomiyaki sauce, mayo, and top with bonito flakes and aonori.

Yaki Tomorokoshi (Grilled Corn with Miso Butter)

Ingredients:

- 2 ears of corn
- 2 tbsp butter, melted
- 1 tbsp white miso
- 1 tbsp soy sauce
- 1 tsp mirin

Instructions:

1. Mix butter, miso, soy sauce, and mirin.
2. Grill corn over medium heat, turning occasionally.
3. Brush with miso butter in the last 2 minutes of grilling.

Teppanyaki Garlic Shrimp

Ingredients:

- 1 lb shrimp, peeled and deveined
- 2 tbsp soy sauce
- 1 tbsp sake
- 1 tbsp mirin
- 1 tbsp garlic, minced
- 1 tbsp butter

Instructions:

1. Marinate shrimp in soy sauce, sake, mirin, and garlic for 15 minutes.
2. Heat a teppan grill or flat-top pan and melt butter.
3. Grill shrimp for 2–3 minutes per side until cooked through.

Yakisoba (Grilled Stir-Fried Noodles)

Ingredients:

- 1 pack yakisoba noodles
- 1/2 cup sliced cabbage
- 1/4 cup sliced carrots
- 1/4 cup sliced bell peppers
- 1/4 cup sliced pork or chicken
- 2 tbsp yakisoba sauce
- 1 tbsp soy sauce
- 1 tsp sesame oil

Instructions:

1. Heat a grill pan or teppan and add sesame oil.
2. Stir-fry meat, then add vegetables.
3. Add noodles and mix in yakisoba sauce and soy sauce.
4. Cook for 3–4 minutes, stirring frequently.

Japanese-Style BBQ Lamb Chops

Ingredients:

- 4 lamb chops
- 2 tbsp soy sauce
- 1 tbsp sake
- 1 tbsp miso paste
- 1 tbsp honey
- 1 tsp grated garlic
- 1 tsp grated ginger

Instructions:

1. Mix soy sauce, sake, miso, honey, garlic, and ginger.
2. Marinate lamb chops for at least 2 hours.
3. Grill over medium-high heat for 3–4 minutes per side.

Sesame Soy Grilled Asparagus

Ingredients:

- 1 bunch asparagus
- 2 tbsp soy sauce
- 1 tbsp sesame oil
- 1 tbsp mirin
- 1 tsp toasted sesame seeds

Instructions:

1. Toss asparagus in soy sauce, sesame oil, and mirin.
2. Grill over medium heat for 2–3 minutes per side.
3. Sprinkle with sesame seeds before serving.

Grilled Daikon with Soy Sauce and Bonito Flakes

Ingredients:

- 1 daikon radish, peeled and sliced into 1/2-inch rounds
- 2 tbsp soy sauce
- 1 tbsp mirin
- 1 tsp grated ginger
- 1 tbsp bonito flakes

Instructions:

1. Steam or boil daikon slices for 5 minutes until slightly tender.
2. Grill over medium heat for 3–4 minutes per side, brushing with soy sauce and mirin.
3. Top with grated ginger and bonito flakes.

Shabu Shabu Grilled Pork Belly Wraps

Ingredients:

- 1/2 lb thinly sliced pork belly
- 1 cup shredded lettuce or cabbage
- 1/4 cup ponzu sauce
- 1 tbsp sesame oil

Instructions:

1. Grill pork belly slices for 1–2 minutes per side until crispy.
2. Serve wrapped in lettuce with ponzu sauce for dipping.

Japanese-Style BBQ Duck Breast

Ingredients:

- 1 duck breast, scored
- 2 tbsp soy sauce
- 1 tbsp sake
- 1 tbsp mirin
- 1 tbsp honey
- 1 tsp grated garlic

Instructions:

1. Mix soy sauce, sake, mirin, honey, and garlic. Marinate duck for 1 hour.
2. Grill skin-side down over medium heat for 6–8 minutes, then flip and cook for 4 more minutes.
3. Let rest for 5 minutes before slicing.

Gyudon-Style Grilled Beef Bowl

Ingredients:

- 1 lb thinly sliced beef (ribeye or sirloin)
- 1/4 cup soy sauce
- 2 tbsp mirin
- 2 tbsp sake
- 1 tbsp sugar
- 1 tsp grated ginger
- 1 clove garlic, minced
- 1 onion, sliced
- 2 bowls steamed rice
- 1 green onion, sliced
- 1 tsp sesame seeds

Instructions:

1. Mix soy sauce, mirin, sake, sugar, ginger, and garlic. Marinate beef for 30 minutes.
2. Grill beef over medium-high heat for 1–2 minutes per side.
3. Sauté onions on the grill pan until soft, then mix with beef.
4. Serve over rice, topped with green onions and sesame seeds.

Yakionigiri with Spicy Tuna Topping (Grilled Rice Balls with Spicy Tuna)

Ingredients:

- 2 cups cooked Japanese rice
- 1/4 cup soy sauce
- 1 tbsp mirin
- 1/2 cup chopped raw tuna
- 2 tbsp mayonnaise
- 1 tbsp sriracha or spicy mentaiko
- 1 tsp sesame oil
- 1 sheet nori, cut into strips

Instructions:

1. Shape rice into triangular balls.
2. Mix soy sauce and mirin, then brush on rice balls.
3. Grill over medium heat for 2 minutes per side until crispy.
4. Mix tuna, mayo, sriracha, and sesame oil.
5. Top grilled rice balls with spicy tuna and garnish with nori strips.

Sansho Pepper Grilled Chicken Thighs

Ingredients:

- 2 boneless chicken thighs
- 1/2 tsp sea salt
- 1/2 tsp ground sansho pepper
- 1 tbsp soy sauce
- 1 tsp sake
- 1 tsp mirin

Instructions:

1. Mix soy sauce, sake, mirin, salt, and sansho pepper. Marinate chicken for 30 minutes.
2. Grill over medium-high heat for 6–7 minutes per side until crispy.

Gochujang-Miso BBQ Glaze for Meats

Ingredients:

- 2 tbsp white miso
- 1 tbsp gochujang (Korean chili paste)
- 1 tbsp soy sauce
- 1 tbsp mirin
- 1 tbsp honey
- 1 clove garlic, grated
- 1 tsp sesame oil

Instructions:

1. Mix all ingredients into a smooth glaze.
2. Brush on meats (beef, chicken, or pork) while grilling.

Spicy Mentaiko Mayo Grilled Seafood

Ingredients:

- 1/2 cup raw shrimp, scallops, or squid
- 2 tbsp spicy mentaiko (pollock roe)
- 2 tbsp mayonnaise
- 1 tsp soy sauce
- 1 tsp lemon juice

Instructions:

1. Mix mentaiko, mayo, soy sauce, and lemon juice.
2. Grill seafood for 2–3 minutes per side.
3. Brush with spicy mentaiko mayo in the last minute of grilling.

Teppanyaki-Style Garlic Butter Vegetables

Ingredients:

- 1 cup sliced zucchini
- 1/2 cup mushrooms
- 1/2 cup bell peppers
- 1 tbsp butter
- 1 clove garlic, minced
- 1 tbsp soy sauce

Instructions:

1. Heat butter and garlic on a flat-top grill or pan.
2. Add vegetables and stir-fry for 4–5 minutes.
3. Drizzle with soy sauce before serving.

Japanese BBQ Glazed Eggplant Skewers

Ingredients:

- 2 Japanese eggplants, sliced into thick rounds
- 2 tbsp soy sauce
- 1 tbsp mirin
- 1 tbsp honey
- 1 tsp sesame oil
- 1 tsp grated ginger

Instructions:

1. Mix soy sauce, mirin, honey, sesame oil, and ginger.
2. Thread eggplant onto skewers and grill for 2–3 minutes per side, brushing with glaze.

Grilled Mochi with Sweet Soy Sauce (Yaki Mochi)

Ingredients:

- 4 pieces store-bought mochi
- 2 tbsp soy sauce
- 1 tbsp sugar
- 1 tbsp mirin
- 1 sheet nori, cut into strips

Instructions:

1. Mix soy sauce, sugar, and mirin into a glaze.
2. Grill mochi over medium heat for 2 minutes per side until crispy.
3. Brush with glaze and wrap with nori.

Wasabi-Soy Grilled Ahi Tuna

Ingredients:

- 1 lb ahi tuna steak
- 2 tbsp soy sauce
- 1 tbsp wasabi paste
- 1 tbsp mirin
- 1 tbsp sesame oil
- 1 tsp grated ginger

Instructions:

1. Mix soy sauce, wasabi, mirin, sesame oil, and ginger. Marinate tuna for 15 minutes.
2. Grill over high heat for 1–2 minutes per side for a rare center.
3. Slice and serve with additional wasabi-soy sauce.

Teriyaki Lamb Skewers

Ingredients:

- 1 lb lamb, cut into cubes
- 1/4 cup soy sauce
- 2 tbsp mirin
- 2 tbsp sake
- 1 tbsp honey
- 1 tsp grated ginger
- 1 clove garlic, minced

Instructions:

1. Mix soy sauce, mirin, sake, honey, ginger, and garlic into a marinade.
2. Marinate lamb cubes for at least 1 hour.
3. Thread onto skewers and grill over medium-high heat for 3–4 minutes per side, brushing with leftover marinade.

Grilled Chicken Gizzard Skewers (Sunagimo Yakitori)

Ingredients:

- 1 lb chicken gizzards, cleaned and cut in half
- 2 tbsp soy sauce
- 1 tbsp sake
- 1 tbsp mirin
- 1/2 tsp salt
- 1/2 tsp black pepper
- Lemon wedges (for serving)

Instructions:

1. Mix soy sauce, sake, mirin, salt, and pepper. Toss gizzards and let sit for 15 minutes.
2. Thread onto skewers and grill over medium-high heat for 3–4 minutes per side.
3. Serve with lemon wedges.

Miso-Marinated Grilled Tofu Steaks

Ingredients:

- 1 block firm tofu, cut into thick slices
- 2 tbsp white miso paste
- 1 tbsp mirin
- 1 tbsp soy sauce
- 1 tsp sesame oil

Instructions:

1. Pat tofu dry and brush with miso, mirin, soy sauce, and sesame oil. Let marinate for 30 minutes.
2. Grill over medium heat for 3–4 minutes per side.
3. Serve with extra sesame seeds and green onions.

Charred Green Peppers with Bonito Flakes (Yaki Piman)

Ingredients:

- 4 Japanese shishito or green bell peppers
- 1 tbsp soy sauce
- 1 tsp sesame oil
- 1/4 cup bonito flakes

Instructions:

1. Grill whole peppers over high heat until blistered, about 2–3 minutes per side.
2. Drizzle with soy sauce and sesame oil.
3. Sprinkle with bonito flakes before serving.

Japanese BBQ Ramen with Smoked Pork

Ingredients:

- 1 lb smoked pork shoulder or belly
- 2 packs fresh ramen noodles
- 4 cups pork broth
- 1/4 cup soy sauce
- 2 tbsp mirin
- 1 tbsp sake
- 1 tsp grated garlic
- 1/2 tsp sesame oil
- 1 boiled egg, halved
- 1 green onion, chopped

Instructions:

1. Heat broth and mix with soy sauce, mirin, sake, garlic, and sesame oil.
2. Slice smoked pork and sear on a hot grill for 1 minute per side.
3. Cook ramen noodles according to package instructions.
4. Serve ramen in broth, topped with smoked pork, boiled egg, and green onions.

Smoked Bonito with Citrus Soy Glaze

Ingredients:

- 1 bonito fillet (or mackerel)
- 1/4 cup soy sauce
- 2 tbsp yuzu or lemon juice
- 1 tbsp mirin
- 1 tbsp honey
- 1 tsp grated ginger

Instructions:

1. Mix soy sauce, yuzu juice, mirin, honey, and ginger into a glaze.
2. Smoke bonito over low heat (225°F) for 30 minutes.
3. Brush with glaze and grill for 1–2 minutes per side before serving.

www.ingramcontent.com/pod-product-compliance
Lightning Source LLC
LaVergne TN
LVHW081340060526
838201LV00055B/2757